ABSENCE OF WINGS

Caitlin Press Inc.
3375 Ponderosa Way
Qualicum Beach, BC V9K 2J8
www.caitlinpress.com

Text and cover design by Vici Johnstone
Edited by Susan Olding
Printed in Canada

Caitlin Press Inc. acknowledges financial support from the Government of Canada and the Canada Council for the Arts, and the Province of British Columbia through the British Columbia Arts Council and the Book Publisher's Tax Credit.

Library and Archives Canada Cataloguing in Publication

Absence of wings / Arleen Paré.
Paré, Arleen, 1946- author.
Poems.
Canadiana 20230203442 | ISBN 9781773861234 (softcover)
LCC PS8631.A7425 A77 2023 | DDC C811/.6—dc23

Absence of Wings

poems

Arleen Paré

Caitlin Press 2023

For A., and for her mother and her sister,
and for all the world's defenceless children

Contents

In 1985 my sister adopted A., an eight-year-old child from Brazil, her new daughter. I became her new daughter's aunt, her only aunt. And I became her mother's main—maybe her only—confidant. *Absence of Wings* bears witness to A.'s story, partial and partially fictionized, and to the profound effect her life had on the small family around her. She was one child in a world of so many. The time we had with her opened the world to us.

PART ONE

1.

She Arrives Wearing a Wide Purple Coat

the angels have no wings / they come to you wearing / their own clothes
Lucille Clifton

The scent of snow this day is laced
with lemon with leaving layered
somewhere between lonely and love
in the breathtaking air between airport and car
her spiralled arrival

and for A. who has never known the cold
snow smells like confusion like nothing at all hollow
a billow at the back of the throat
April is the month the 13th and yet snow
still falls loosely falling apart
an undersong the last notes of winter folding into the first notes of spring

she arrives wearing a wide purple coat felted wool with a belt
and a tricoloured toque mauve magenta maroon
in the car the hat stays on her head

plus there is this dog small enough but still a dog
on the back seat where A. and the dog must ride side by side
fur-feathered-gold but under its lips teeth
she knows about teeth in Brazil there are dogs that will kill you
ask anyone in São Paulo those dogs will eat you tear you apart

so A. sits tight against the car door eyes angled right
watching out the back window into the white avoiding
the sight of the furred lump with two ears
that could bite her kill her
though its head now lies on its paws

I could call this mythology authentic in part
as mythology sometimes begins in partial truth
wherein an original small human being
grows through tribulation into a god a goddess
the god of endurance let's say
or the god of a very big smile

I'm only her aunt   her new mother's sister
my sister and I talk all the time on the phone
which makes me the long-distant   long-time
confidant   emotional witness

and this is simply a story
of fortitude   partially very partially true
mythopoeic wherever needed   places I couldn't   places
I could only imagine

I know so much
I know so little

The New Mother's Big Sister (a.k.a. the aunt)

I became A.'s new aunt when I saw the small headshot the orphanage has sent to my sister it began then or maybe I didn't see the photo at all maybe my sister simply described A.'s eight-year-old face to me over the phone as she read me the written description hyperactive or maybe they said overactive so much of this story happened over the phone and so long ago

I said find out what they mean by overactive does she fight does she bite I worked in mental health at the time I knew the codes what could be buried in a word like overactive I don't remember what my sister said she wasn't concerned

and I was wrong I didn't understand that once A. her picture once my sister had seen her in the small three-by-five she was smitten no thought no wish to turn back A. was smiling and she needed a home my sister knew she was perfect she knew they were destined

and I was thinking only of my sister younger hold her hand my mother told me keep her safe bring her home
my sister was thinking only of A.

in this story I am not even an *eye*witness
I am an ear at the end of the line
an aunt three thousand miles to the west   copper cables   fibre optics
laid along highways and waterways
across farmlands and fields   over and under

our twice-weekly words
worlds
we catch up on the phone
hours
all she can say and all she can't say
that private   that much to protect

I learn
without seeing it takes years of reflection
she day-to-days it in her Ottawa kitchen
in the changeable eye

The New Aunt (a.k.a. the author)

My sister returns from Brazil the 13th of April   and here on the West Coast the day is blue and filled with pink blossoms and with the news that my sister   my younger sister   has returned to Ottawa with her new eight-year-old daughter   safe

When I was five my mother would tell me to take my sister's hand   that tiny five-fingered star   when we'd cross Lakeshore Boulevard   hold her hand my mother would say   and when she played on the street with the older children   when she cried when she'd fight   she was only three

always defiant   bring her home my mother would tell me   keep her safe   hold her hand   bring her home

I visit her on April 29th   west coast to east   to celebrate this blessed arrival   gold frankincense   myrrh

I want this to be factual
but some was never told
even over the phone
so much   so heavily unsaid
even then
how could it otherwise be   so much so heavily unheard

you'll never guess what happened today
and I never could
as I stirred chicken soup on the stove with one hand
holding with the other
the Bakelite receiver tight to my ear
the spiral phone cord stretched to its limit across the small kitchen

so much so heavily heard

there are no cows in these fields   these city fields flitting by
at the side of the highway airport-to-town
no cows no horses no sheep   no feral dogs in the streets
in the streets no dogs on or off leashes   no dogs at all

no monkeys no toucans no nuns in these fields
in these white fields of dissonance   lying flat   lying empty   fleeting by
snow flirting outside the car window

crows yes overhead   shrapnelled against the grey rubbled sky
and two-by-two tail lights winking red the afternoon white
wires   poles   tall buildings layered like colossal cakes
tall wedding cakes
                    A.'s only eight   how would she know
about wedding cakes   she's never seen a wedding   or a layered cake
only puddings white puddings rice puddings blancmange
and black-and-white nuns

her new mother sits in the car directly in front
mid-April and the snow sugar-light
the wind whining its own undertune lifts the pale stuff in dizzying spins
a loose form of free   fluttering as if miniscule birds
A. is entering a strange   a phenomenal swirl
beginning again in this snow globe new world

even jammed against the car door A. is jumped-up   speedy
never unmoving   inside her heart she is restless   can't stop

the Rideau Canal rides by in the form of a narrow ice floor
in those mid-80s the canal froze over till spring
skaters swept south and southwest arm-in-arm cantilevered into the weather
while some skated north or northeast with the push of the wind at their backs

spring '85 arrived late   arrived early May
a few years ago spring came early March
and a dog fell through the ice mid-canal

One April Snowflake (one among many)

I am only one snowflake   one among so many many   we are particular   unique
whole constellations of individuated blur   but still I wanted to save her   she
looked so fragile that day   I wanted to protect her from our cold collective frag-
mentation   trying to avoid falling on her behatted head as she got into the car   I
angled left picking up a slight tail of cold wind   falling then onto the pavement
where I   the whole thing happened so fast

A. stays pinned between seatback and seatbelt
while outside the wind buckles trees   swings overhead signs
suspended on cables above the white road
where sometimes two streets will suddenly
meet

so light she could be a bird   a heron   fine boned and winged
a small heron   not blue   or a lark   she could be a lark   but not meadow
or a small angel   wingless   in a wide purple coat
a hummingbird   she could be a hummingbird   restive
with a ruby-red throat

A.'s new mother is gay   not that A. speaks any English
the new mother does not think of herself as middle-class
nor did she ever intend to give birth
the new mother is Buddhist and white
A. is Catholic and Black

never before this week has A. been in a car
nor inside a plane with two silver wings in a cloud-jumbled sky
never before has she secured a new mother
never been seated this close to a dog
never been on a two-wheeler BMX bike
nor slept in a bed in a room by herself
although inside the orphanage   inside the locked closet
there   behind the locked closet door   darkness
sometimes there in the dark she was made to sleep by herself   on the floor

A. is the beginning   the start   fearless   mostly fearless   and fast
not so much fleeing or fugitive   maybe the word should be saved   we could say
she is saved
rescued from perpetual unpleasant unkindness   from the hem of despair

the pale-yellow grass is covered in places thinly in white
and the hedges are white-lined and leafless

now she is eating orange cheese from a clear plastic bag
salty and soft   the dog sleeps   they slip through the white city
on their way home to the new mother's house
it could be twilight on Mars

I want to say this is more than a story
a mythicism
about a small family
who live safe and protected behind a white picket fence   as in
Father Knows Best   but given the fact of no father   who can know best
and the white picket fence might be white-washed   the paint thinned with turps

in this story I am only the witness   the only one
in this story there are aspirations   there are systems
institutions   decisions   and days filled with angst

how fast the arrival all passed
São Paulo   taxi   hotel   taxi   the airport   the plane
New York City   the airport there when they stopped between flights
my sister said
an armed guard appearing in front or behind or off to the side
to track every one of their movements
ensuring they'd board the plane to the north

The New Mother (a.k.a. my sister)

The problem with racism, well, one of the problems with racism, one of the day-to-day problems, not the massive mayhem problems, not as in George Floyd's murder in broad daylight by big city police, not in which the fabric of the world is rent with bare hands and guns, but one of the day-to-day everyday problems, that kind of problem, is that when a New York airport security guard follows you around with your new eight-year-old daughter as you wait for your connecting flight to the north, to Canada, you can't quite tell whether this is because your new daughter is Black or because she runs too fast through the corridors or because she's adopted and from Brazil. I couldn't tell. I had never been followed that way in an airport. Every time I looked back, he was there, watching.

A. is a whole other language   Brazilian Portuguese
is what she translates
knowing nothing about this new English tongue
its strange arrangements of sounds

time is not simply a clock   not always a friend
nor does it spiral or pivot   counter or spin
it simply moves on   as if it knows where it's going
entering whole other places   each minute in a deft row
nor is each minute always a friend

in the driver's seat the woman's friend drives the car through the blur of traffic and snow
the sky still falling out of itself   soft pieces of cloud
the windshield fogs time to time as if mist   a miasma
time to time the new mother swivels her head   looks back to check A. and the dog
are they getting along
the dog is getting along
not so much A. jammed as she is against the solid
the bitter cold door
the plastic bag now empty in her purple wool lap

2.

Who Rove the Streets of São Paulo, Brazil

You can survive anything if you know that someone is looking out for you
June Beisch

believers in true romance or in preordained lives might say this story is
as if an act of a god in multiple acts   and yes A.'s new mother is
as if an uncommon good godly act

                                    and in the way that one thing can lead
                    to another
A.'s new mother's mother   A.'s grandmother if she had lived
left a concavity   dying   left a niche in the new mother's heart
in her middleclass household with only one dog
that same dog on the backseat   whose name was Poppy
a rescue dog who eats lost sandwiches whenever she finds them
sandwiches gone missing in the dead of winter
ham and Swiss frozen stiff in Irving Street Park

the woman changed Poppy's name from the name Puppy
a nondescript generic   an everyman everywoman medium-sized everydog name
a who-cares kind of name for a dog who lived on a farm
with three hens two pigs and one baby goat
but the dog is not a child   cannot say the word *mother*

plus   ask anyone   one day A. would have been banished
kicked out   aging out of orphanage care   how then could she ever be safe

they shoot children who rove the streets of São Paulo
ask anyone   ask the children   the police
out with their guns in the blistering nights and in blinding middays
in back alleys where unguarded children   all undersized
skitter in scavenging flocks as if city birds   looking for food   trying to hide
disappearing under parked cars

ducking round bins that billow sweet-smelling trash
trying to live   incidental   each one trying
each one a small moving piece of the city

but A. has slipped away from that city   vanished
leaving that unprofitable unprotected probable path
that predestined almost fated future imperfect

What then could be more delightful than snow falling
watched from the shelter of her own purple coat
or more mysterious than a dog with no visible teeth
or more delicious than orange cheese from a clear plastic bag

this much she knows
she is beginning again
in the back seat of an apple-red car

plus there continues even now the traditional generic collective opinion
a certain cooperative unconscious agreement
that it demonstrates social good grace to settle a child into your home
for pure unsullied happiness   at least one

in the same way that a chicken in every pot implies prosperity
even though the new mother does not subscribe to old-fashioned views
being a feminist and a vegetarian
while A. would happily eat a slice of baked ham

and truly the woman has space in her heart for this child
given the world's too-many children with never enough
maybe two if she's lucky   maybe A.'s younger half-sister
who still lives in São Paulo with the black-and-white nuns

A. will lose all the words that now line her brain
will replace them with English translations
despite the new mother's efforts to forestall this linguistic aphasia
this geo-economic socio-cultural erasure of original words
forgetting these words   but not entirely

nor entirely forgetting the times that happened before
some of those black-and-white religiosa were mean
some merely young   some shoved you into a closet   locked the door
whenever whatever   and A. was whenever whatever most of the time
which amounted to too much dark-closet time   trapped

                       ins

                    ide t

                    he dar

                    k close

                    t r

                    ats b

                    ig a

                    s bigc

                    ats

makes sense that she couldn't keep still
so much happened to her there
maybe even before

until my sister   the woman in the flowered green shirt
knocked on the large São Paulo Orfanato front door
and A. hearing the knock   shouted out
as if in reply   waiting there   waiting in the hall for her new mother's knock
and the woman   the new mother outside the door hearing A. shouting
shouting out

> *Essa é minha mãe minha mãe chegou*
>
> *that is my mother   my mother has arrived*

so that even though the woman spoke no Portuguese
the woman knew   almost knew   what A. was shouting
even though she couldn't make out the words
it was not the words

I do not believe that mysticism is necessarily obfuscation
I do not believe that myth always obscures what is true

A. was shouting to the girls in the hall who were waiting there with her
who wished to be waiting for their mothers too
first mothers or new mothers
mothers who would never come to take them away
this is not a story in the *Madeline* tradition of girlhood
not a good-ending fairy tale story   not for them all
ask them   this was real life

A. was standing in the front hall with the high-vaulted ceiling behind the heavy
front door
a gargantuan door
leading into a gargoyle of Greystone   a flaunt of a building   a monolith
with built-in touches of terror   neo-gothic with wings
as if an owl or a goshawk   with long slanted talons
something that could predate   with long slanted shadows
small prey in the wings   trapped   unhinged and unsafe

even then   that first day   A. knew the singular knock of her new singular mother
her second mother
her first mother nowhere she recalled
not even the favela
made all the sense she could make at the time
her brother was then only four when the first mother

A. was two the night the neighbours woke to the frantic
the unstoppable
the crying   no one slept that whole hot unbearable night
in the morning the neighbour called the child welfare
who arrived   the morning already ablaze   and took A. away
her brother too   though her brother where to A. couldn't possibly know
wrapped in a thin square of pale cotton
she was lifted from her damp basket   crying
her spine curving away from the stranger's two hands
when before it was only her mother's two hands

her brother in his thin   his only brown shorts

ask anyone   A. was a fierce force of nature   even then
she never stopped

what is the word for moving without obvious motion
controlled   caged   some form of rage?

what papers were signed when they took her away
where was the first mother that night and the day before too
where was she now   what   who   kept her from the favela those long-ago nights
from A. and her brother   from her small home of cardboard and tin

a hospital bed   a prison cell   an edifice built to detain
that mother who might talk to herself in the streets or fight back

in the swarm of those São Paulo streets
in the midst of those long-ago   complex   those abandonment days

A. is still holding the clear plastic bag
when the woman the new mother
opens the back seat car door
unhooks A.'s seatbelt   and A. gets out of the car
and Poppy
jumps out onto the driveway   jumping in front
almost knocking A. onto the still-frosted street

The undersigned Sworn Translator of the English language, duly qualified, appointed and commissioned in and for the City and State of São Paulo, does hereby certify that a document written in the Portuguese language was presented to her in order to be translated into English, which she has done in her official capacity, to wit:--

JUDICIARY, São Paulo--

Process No 383/84-3/NO (50/78/CRN)--

Matter heard in court, etc.--

█████████, duly qualified in the above mentioned court files, has applied for the simple adoptnat [sic] an ██████████████████, female, born December 8, 1976, in this Capital City of São Paulo, State of São Paulo, to ██████████████ (page 38 of said file), who was summoned to court (page 74) and heard (page 78).

Considering the report on page 85 of said file, a Special Curator was appointed, and his opinion given (page 88).

The minor child was adjudicated to be in an irregular situation (i.e. abandonment) (page 26), and her mother's parental rights terminated (page 89).

The social worker's report supports the granting of adoption (page 127/155), and the Curator of Minors' opinion given on page 172/back of said file.

NOW, THEREFORE, I hereby RESOLVE:

The minor child has been institutionalized at "Associação Casa de Criança Santa Terezinha" for about five years, has not been visited by her mother, which confirms her abandonment.

The applicant parent has fulfilled all legal requirements for adoption, is competent, healthy, thirty years old, as evidenced by the coments [sic] submitted to this court.

However, I find it advisable to establish a probation period, during which time the adjustment of both parties will be observed.

Thus, I hereby grant guardianship of ███████████████ to the applicant parent, pursuant to article 26 of the Code of Minors, and article 412 of the Civil Code.

I hereby release the party from any legal pledge, as reportedly said child owns no property.

I hereby establish a probation period of six months, as of the execution of the Sentence of Guardianship, which shall be issued after the filing of the homestudy prepared by the Adoption Agency.

I hereby order a Travel License be issued, so that child may travel abroad.

São Paulo, January 16, 1985

(signed) ███████████████

    Judge and Acting Judge of Minors

(from mother's records)

3.

She Takes up the Whole Screen

A. lands in this new city at a time of too much
interest rates in two digits
Grace Jones singing
loud   her generous voice
her shoulders wide as the world
her hair cropped on her sleek good-looking
her movie-star head
everyone is loving Grace Jones
she takes up the whole screen

Louis Armstrong has already died
but his music
his wonderful world
singing on

O São Paulo Orfanato   Catholic and riven with crosses of silver
white wimples   black beads   wide-skirted nuns
do you miss little A.'s capricious spirit   capacious
spacious as those doublewide halls?

what is the word for running when there's no place to go

do you regret the excessive restraints
rue the hubris BS to keep her in check?
what rules applied to her
and not to the others?
what castigations?

husha o husha who has not fallen down?

the new mother   my sister
                                        may she never fall down

Re: ████████████████████

Type of Child

████████████████████ is a very beautiful and very bright girl. She is sponta-
neous with others, outgoing, and friendly. She is very popular with both adults
and children, and has a good-natured spirit. Basically, she is a happy person, and
a leader among her friends. It appears that she is a natural athlete, with abilities
far beyond others her age, particularly in the area of gymnastics. She also enjoys
signing, dancing, and swimming.

Her summer holidays were spent partly at an English as a second language
school for children, and we also went on many outings to beaches, my family's
cottage, parks, and various other excursions.

Schooling, Language Acquisition

She has just started back to school…

(by mother, from mother's records)

Report from the Social Worker in Brazil (Inez Perez Moroz)

According to facts from FEBEM [A. and her brother] were authorized for adoption placement on the base of a psychiatric report from hospital Vila M which diagnosed her [the mother] as [ill] and her rights were terminated on April 14, 1982.

(from mother's records)

the '80s   those years of Teflon and tolerance
a decade of turbulent hyperactivities   financial transactions
when long distant phone calls still cost by the minute
and yet we still call   for hours we talk

Staying Alive   shoulder pads and the promise of full human rights
hippies buying their way into the burbs   the '80s changing everything
for the new mother too
blueprints of brick-coloured hope   cheap flights to Fiji
(but not Chile   where no one will go   the killings there   and the ongoing bloody)

baby boomers with bank accounts drinking wine from vineyards in France
and the lush Napa Valley   though not from the boycotted
apartheided South African state where Pretoria has murdered
Steve Biko who never could agree to give up his mind

stock markets boom   the Dow Jones is at 20 percent
the consummate rise of unkind corporations

men in Canada can no longer legally rape their own wives
blueberry yogurt sells for 2 dollars a tub

A.'s new mother's grandfather was born out of wedlock
nineteenth century   raised in a barn   his own mother never did
never could   save him
or save herself
from those old-County-Antrim-marital-adjacent-farm-family-traditions

many have died   the world's sorrows
still bleed across countries
bodies   and bodies of water

immediately   the six words my sister spoke into the phone
when I told her he was born out of wedlock

                                        I've always felt like an outsider

The New Mother's Grandfather (a.k.a. Tom)

You've got this new-fangled notion these days: "epigenetics." Five syllables and a stack of books and I could'a told you all about it myself when I was alive. See, for instance, if Paddy's a drunk, and Christ knows Paddy's the worst, then sure, Paddy's father must'a been a drunk too, old Liam, and he was. And Liam's father as well. Liam couldn't rise most mornings till well after eight. Almost missed his own wedding. Goes all the way back to Adam, who must 'a been Irish. Makes sense: think of the weight on that poor man's new shoulders, one rib missing and his wife cavorting with snakes under the tree. Plus all the cider there in the garden free for the taking.

On down to Paddy's son Michael who turns sixteen in a week and will start drinking the very day he turns if he hasn't already, and carry on every night like a traditional trout. His own son wading in the watery wings.

I blame the English, their Cromwell, their queen, their high and their mighty. I'd rather shake the hand of Old Nick hisself.

As for me, sure and I drink, but not so bad what with the line being bent and me raised up in the barn. My son Tom favours his mother, never took to the drink, sides with her every damn time. The exception that proves. Or would that be simple genetics on his dear mother's side? And what of deracination? How does that fit with the whole ball of wax?

4.

The Absence of Wings

Time arrows on and Poppy is not a puppy at all anymore
is now very old for a dog and will die   and a new dog
a silver-coloured Weimaraner named Kuska
will arrive in the home
be installed in Poppy's old bed

night always falls   no one can halt the full length of dark
though time itself makes no sense   ask Einstein
ask Einstein's wife

how much time even in the foggiest sense
will it take   how much faith
who knows how to gird her
the mother
guard her
the daughter
advise them
what to expect in this city of briefcases and suits
blond hair and blue eyes
how to manage
the privileged
the predominant fray
before the knock on the door her life was even then
unbeknownst   beginning again

the day of the Home Study Report
a tall man with wire-rimmed glasses
and a faux-leather briefcase
clipboard and pen
and a list of official home-study questions
which the woman would answer with no hesitation

he queried through her two-storey home   bouncing beds
opening the fridge to check the shining white shelves
blueberry yogurt   orange juice   a jug of two percent milk
check
       check
           check
testing a pear from the porcelain bowl   pale and unblemished
noting the paintings   trees   birds and lakes   on the apple-green living-room walls
returning at last to his cup of tea cooling on the pine table

The Home-Study Worker (Les Bolton)

Yes pretty colours rose and pale green hand-knotted rugs a bookcase with proper good books yes a colour TV true she applied as a one-parent family but she passed the conditions food in the fridge a bank account no criminal past she smiled at the dog that lay at her feet the whole time

True I prefer the traditional two-parent-white-picket-fence-mum-and-dad-situation but she easily passed International Adoption she made me a nice cup of tea in the mid-afternoon good luck to them all

1983

Letter from the Ontario Ministry of Community and Social Services, Children's Services Branch, Community Services Division, Toronto, to the Canada Immigration Centre Ottawa

Dear Sirs:

Re: Adoption of A.

Born: December 8, 1976, in Brazil

by (the woman, the new mother)

Comfort Street, Ottawa, Ontario

A favourable report has been received from the Children's Aid Society of Ottawa-Carleton.

The report indicates that the sponsor is financially secure and able to offer a good home to A.

There is no objection to the permanent transfer of A. from Brazil to the home of (the new mother).

Yours sincerely,

Agnes Goodfellow

(from mother's records)

A.'s younger half-sister will arrive in a year and a half
and will be her real sister half-sister and the woman will be
her half-sister's real mother too

A. is eight going on nine   her half-sister is now three almost four
the word in Portuguese is *adotar*

her sister will be almost five when she reaches this capital city
via the mountains of paper and ink

and the snow
                will have fallen again and again   and again

beginning again   backing up   way back   without looking back
the Angel of History

her half-sister will arrive on a 747 the same way as A.
from São Paulo Brazil
same orphanage but from the third floor

when her four-year-old half-sister arrives   late '86
the dog is or is not Poppy   I can't say for certain
nor can I say the month   or whether the half-sister knows
that A. is her half-sister too   her *meia-irmã*

she is small and wears a pink skirt

These are the two international daughters of the new intentional mother
They are the perfect   the sisters
who fill the near-perfect house
and fill the now-not-so-new mother's big heart

the half-sister attends the neighbourhood school
grade one with some children from other countries who speak
almost no English
and some other kids born in this country speaking English all their short lives

and one   this one kid   a joker   who makes his bad stupid joke—*ha ha*—
that the sister's sweet hands are made out of sh**
who can think this is funny   do the other kids laugh?

this is Canada   the mother complains to the teacher who claims
there is nothing she   the teacher   can do   she throws up her hands
it's only grade one
what about racism
there is a principal who recites *kids will be kids*
can he be as racist as the new mother's own father?
1987 and there is nothing the school is able   they say   is willing to do

this is beginning   again and again
Are those your own children?
asks a woman in the cereal aisle
her daughters both looking away

A.'s now mother is at this time aged thirty-six   thirty-six
will become the significant number   there are significant numbers
and composite numbers
prime numbers and unnatural numbers
and thirty-six is a natural number
adding up to nine which they say
recommends love
to the world

they say nine implies
                    consciousness of a certain international kind

and if nine is the natural congruent number
then attachment and love
                              across borders and marrows
will be the natural congruent answer

A. will be thirty-six when she takes her last breath.

These are the days they will have
the years of A. and her new mother together
iridescent
                incandescent luminescent
                                            halcyon days

as if they could ever be cleaved
                                one from the other

ever since her mother-to-be first studied the small three-by-five snap
of the sweet-looking child
despite written insinuations concerning A.'s overactive behaviours
ever since the woman first knocked on the oversized Orfanata front door
loud as heart's yearning

ever since A. announced her new mother's arrival
loud very loud
ever since   nothing could stop this tributary
this triumphal flow

snow will cover much of the domestic historical present and past
these cold northern streets will sparkle with ice
glittering new frost in the morning in this glimmer-gloss city

these are the days of global adoption
international home-studied transnational mothers
of children who once knew nothing of snow

the woman at first thought maybe India
her friend had adopted a child from the shores of Korea

I once knew a woman who found newborn twin girls
from an overwrought mother of six in the Romanian hills
so small she could hold each infant in the palm of a hand

world population in 1985 approaching five billion
now over eight

the woman is knocking on the front door   reverberating
percussing
as if striking a drum

A. is shouting inside
the door abounding with sound
in a whole other tongue

so loud the new mother can hear
the burl of A.'s voice   her about-to-be daughter
through the thick purple heartwood

Sister Maria Obligata

A. was aquela garota era tão rapida, so fast, she was always so fast. As if a cheetah. But she sang like a passáro. Such a thin little bird but with a plentiful voice.

Sister Florenca Unfortunata

But she pulled at our habits, our skirts, yanked on our aprons, our rosary beads, which have been blessed and are sacred. We wrote "energetic" on the agency form plain as we could. Always spinning, whirling, a dervish, always whirling; she was maybe Old Nick herself.

The new mother now alone in the midst of this might this mercurial child

There were times early on when A. wanted
needed to locate her unlocatable self
latitude longitude north south sky land snow grass night day
Black white English Brazilian Portuguese

but all she had was the woman
they became very close

                      the new mother (my sister)
                              became A.'s new polar star

no one now will kill A. in the streets of São Paulo
she is no longer there for the killing

The Author (a.k.a. A.'s mother's older sister)

I have said to my sister over the phone in my helpless hubris   oh no oh no   over and over again

you need a counsellor   gripping the phone   beige now hanging on the white wall

has she

will you

will she

together or alone

or alone

then try a different counsellor

will you let the school know

write the letter   talk to the teacher

harassment   almost harassment   my ventured solutions   advise advise   so burden-some   free

take her hand   keep her safe   bring her home

fixing this fixing that fixing A. fixing her fixing me

some days I can barely stomach my own solving self

where are they   those nuns
                              with their looping black beads
clack-clacking the sides of their voluminous skirts
                              crosses silvering their black-and-white chests

where are the orphans with their bare unintentional shins
                              where are their mothers
their first disappeared

and the police
            waiting there
                        behind buildings
                              on corners

their number-nine Lugers
the sound of their boots
their knee-high official issue black leather boots
polished like mirrors
heavy-heeled and steel-toed

5.

One Child among Many

nothing / innocent is safe
Lucille Clifton

years ago   when we were young   that old orphanage on Côte de Liesse
one stone
on top
of another
four storeys high   that much we could see

when we were young   nine and seven   my sister and I would swivel our heads to
the left
driving north with our parents
as we passed that stony grey building   craning our necks to see down the lane
the long tree-lined lane   to the faraway end where the orphanage
that large   a blurry ghost of a place on Côte de Liesse

Notre Dame de Liesse   meaning jubilation   our lady of
with hundreds of children inside its walls   children under
the care of the Catholic Church   under   that kind of care   we saw only the walls

The children there were known then as "Duplessis Orphans"
the '40s   the '50s   that time of Great Darkness
Premier Duplessis in official loco parentis for almost in total twenty-one thousand
deliberately   conveniently   mis-
certified mentally incompetent $1.25 for each mistreated abandoned poor child
Federal cash flowing   year after misleading year   child after mislabeled child
increasing provincial coffers   no sign of jubilation for miles around

One of Duplessis Mid-Century Orphans

—Louis-Joseph Hébert; a.k.a. Nestor

When you [are] a bastard… [it's like] being born in a garbage can.

turn of the last last century   18s to 19s   growing these big social ideas leading then
to big buildings for those unable   those dispossessed   those perhaps miscertified
misdiagnosed and yes

humane was the new big building idea   instead of the former backalleysbasement-
sorattics   places where rats   but

big plans big ideas do not assure the humane

the American Kirkbride Plan   blueprinting   prototyping new institutions
stepped linear
                    footprints
                                        staggered wings spreading
                                        the wingspans of hawks

each housing two-hundred-and-fifty   at least
asylums   orphanages   hospitals   prisons
architectural buttresses
set on acres of grass with big trees and big sky
the grass always green
the sky always cloudless clear azure blue

there were one-hundred-and-thirty Indian Residential Schools
over that twentieth century
                        when the last closed it was already 1996

when A. sat in the apple red car that snowy day in 1985
tight against the car door
hundreds of children sat in those residential school classrooms
tight in their small wooden desks
against their young wills
but how much will
can one child ever wield

and against the wills of their parents and their grandparents
their aunties ancestors into infinity

sitting there eating working weeping
not speaking
their own language not even a word

Caughnawaga Indian Day School for instance
outside Montreal run by the Oblates of Mary
Immaculate and Pointe Bleue Indian Residential
School not closed until 1965

St. Margaret's Indian Residential
School Fort Frances Ontario closing in '74 after seventy-two years

and school graves more than three thousand children died
in those schools more than buried there in the backyards more than

Sept-Îles Indian Residential School in Sept-Îles Quebec
closing in '67
Poplar Hill Indian Residential School in Poplar Hill First Nation Ontario
still running in '85 when A. stepped out of the car

all the children in all those grey buildings
nuns at their heels   brothers and priests   belts in their fists
blinders at their blue-blinded eyes
rung round by children
wild-eyed with hunger
confusion and fear   blancmange and potatoes
barley   red apples and dread

three thousand   more than three thousand
their bright their beautiful   their names buried too

Indian Girl No. 237
so many
tiny school graves
unseen   named or unnamed   completely unsung

Sœur Maria Magdalena of the Oblates of Mary Immaculate

I was young then, too young to teach in those classrooms, which is no excuse, I know. I could not understand what I was expected to do, what the children needed. I had young brothers and sisters at home. They obeyed me because I was the eldest, but I had two parents too.

I'm old now, and mea culpa mea culpa, I don't expect forgiveness, no hope of ever forgiving my own unforgivable self.

snow covers the sidewalk   covers the cars
layers white the fine branches
as if the branches were cloaked now with lunar moth wings

her memory of heat is an underground ache
ghosts of her brother   first mother   first bed
a closet betraying no incoming light
dark as the night at times of no moon
an afterimage
of her unfledged
her yet unproven life

Snow is visible wind. It blows with a vociferous voice.

6.

How Fast a Life

Bank Street and next a short street called Aylmer
beginning again   1985   and this chronicular sequence moving
slowly   or is it too fast
and not always in a perfect straight line

a sharp turn to the right   a stoplight in red   a go-light in green

the glass at A.'s cheek is still cold as an ache
and still the dog sleeps
too close to her thin purple hip

sky blurred as churned water
sky high in the corner of A.'s freezing eye
a small piece of sky very small very bluing
moving
in an almost straight line

how fast it all passes São Paulo taxi hotel taxi the airport the plane
New York City the airport there when they stopped between flights
the armed guard appearing to track them
ensuring they'd board the next plane to the north

and the wind and the dead-looking trees
car dog all sifting seeming ordained a jigsaw
a story of fracture
how lives pulled apart might later fix back together or not
tessellations and consolations

we want this to be fabrication but this is the not the right word
A. was reaching for joy and her new mother reaching hands spread
to loosen mistakes historical hurtful hierarchical wrongs
piece by piece fitting into new patterns
shifting almost intact

the whole house about to transform
for one thing A. cannot stop moving even when she stops
she can't stop what is the word for running while
staying in the same place

but wait
the snow furls the car stops the sun
shines of a sudden
the dog has eaten no one but now might be hungry

A. is now alone with the woman in the woman's enormous white house
she throws off her wide purple coat kicks off her shoes
fingers her clear plastic bag with no cheese remaining
the house is shiny all bright and glassy
with no other children in sight

and the woman is now on her own with the unstoppable A.
who now will sleep through the whole night

faint dreams of trees A. once knew in Brazil
as she falls finally to sleep memories
lesser animals common birds a whole sky of dark noise

in the locked closet of the old Orfanato the Casa de Crianza
there were always faint skitters
mice maybe a large rat maybe more
cockroaches scratching words on the walls
where hanging on hooks
were broom handles and mops

in the orphanage courtyard in those once-before days
were toucans and tanagers cherry-throated red-necked scarlet macaw
glaucous and hyacinth thrush rufous-bellied
and the blue-eyed ground dove
was it there that she learned the language of birds

possum under the hedges short-tailed

and once a three-banded hard-shelled armadillo

and monkeys on the stone walls and monkeys in trees
black squirrel and brown howler
spider brown capuchin marmoset common
sometimes not uncommonly
dead on the path

Sister Maria Antonio Pugnacia

Of course we had to kill the monkeys because of the yellow fever. We laid poison down on the path. In the morning sometimes they would be there. Sometimes the children saw them like that. They should know this is part of life.

Sister Santa Barbara Brutalus

We had to discipline all the children at all times, these girls from the streets, the favelas, some were brutes. Girls, but some bit. Imagine, some even bit us. Girls. There was no way but to discipline them at all times. A. was from Favela Alba, not an easy girl, always moving, loud, snatching food. So fast. This is what all the sisters had to manage. At all times. We had to have special rules for A. Of course. Moving. At all times she was moving. Was A. the worst? I would say maybe she was almost the worst, although Sister Cecelia Obligata, the choir mistress, loved to hear her sing. Like a bird, she said. I prefer the voices of toucans.

not that the nuclear family is a perfect solution
not that it's not famously flawed   famously nuclear
ask anyone   ask Einstein
energy cannot be created nor can it be fully destroyed
though it can shift   neuroplasticity
the spread of the vast Milky Way   and yet

she did not have to be perfect
that she had arrived was perfection enough
the woman had waited over two years
so long she began to fear that no children
were left in the world to adopt

so many children   so few to adopt
the way some people go hungry
while others forsake their ham sandwiches
in Irving Street Park

that freak April snowfall   almost a blizzard
turning later that day to sunshine by four
perfection enough   it was Ottawa
A. walked into the house with hooked rugs and a colour TV

before the woman opened the door   the woman
my sister   was already a new mother   perfect   unpractised
and A. was already her new perfect unpractised daughter

with no expectations no nostalgia no pity no tears
she began all over again

she had memories   ghosts flying
becoming untethered   wings   becoming unfeathered

PART TWO

1.

With No Good Place to Land

in the despoiled and radiant now
Stephen Dunn

And then there is this sudden not so sudden unexpected slide as if someone had just upended a table her life in slow motion and everything on the table starts to slide off and the life of her family everything with no good place to land

Elsewhere:
São Paulo   twenty girls waking up in a dorm where A.
just a few days before   slept
6 a.m.   every morning the bell

despite the time difference   the flight   the car ride   and the new sleeping arrange-
ments
first night in the new city   A. sleeps through the whole cold Ottawa night

the mother will call her sister the next morning three hours away
where the sister is stirring porridge with dried fruit and raw nuts

we slept through the night says the mother
not a peep   but she slept on the floor
and now she won't eat the cream of wheat that I've made
and she is drinking my coffee right now as I speak

try toast says the aunt   I can't help myself   *with strawberry jam*

Elsewhere:
California   gay men are dying of AIDS   drug addicts too
evangelicals proclaim the wrath of their god
proclaims the announcer on the CBC mid-morning news
the day will be sunny   the radio claims   no more snow till next year

Elsewhere:
America   Ronald Reagan smiles his tight all-American teeth
into his all-American second term
all the while losing his mind
all the while Reaganomics
loosing safety nets all over the world

Elsewhere:
Nairobi   The International Women's Conference
planning the massive event
global feminism spreading
its fervent wings

Meanwhile:
Ottawa   A. goes to school wearing her purple wool hat
the whole month of May
shifts in her desk in a classroom with nine rectangular windows along the fourth
wall
the desk's top rides smoothly on hinges   up and down   up and down
she roams through the classroom   this sweet whirlwind girl
up and down   up and down   round and round

at home she wolfs bowls of orange mac and cheese

weekends she races through Irving Street Park
the golden dog at her rubber-soled heels
runs rings round the pet

evenings she bathes in a white porcelain tub water puddling the bathroom floor
tiles

she pages the books that her mother reads her at night
prefers the bright pictures of birds

these are the days of fortune and silvered salvation
one day her younger half-sister will come

2.

No Fairy Tale Curse

in May my sister takes A. to meet our elderly father
by affiliation A.'s new grandfather
though to be honest this new grandfather finds it a stretch
to be grandfathered with no prior notice
without the intervening conventional nine-month gestation
with no consultation at all

maybe also for A. a stretch maybe for the new mother too

when our mother died
our father the new grandfather took a new wife

the new wife is younger
and she can cook

The New Grandfather (a.k.a. Tom, named after his father the Great-Grandfather)

I told her when she brought the kid to the condo. My second wife, Sophie, was there. Someone had to tell her: She'll ruin your life, I told her. "Sophie," I said, "What do you think?" I don't know what Sophie replied, she was in the kitchen fixing our lunch. I'm not a racist. I was just telling the straightforward truth.

And wait, let's get this part straight too. That bit from my father some pages back, him saying he wasn't much of a drinker. Baloney. Whiskey, no ice. For the record, he drank too much and he drank too often. Ask my mother. Even she had to admit. Whenever we'd visit their flat in Verdun, Sundays, him saying to my two little girls, here, handing them his glass, as if they would know what to do, laughing, taste it, taste it. My wife, my first wife who died—broke my heart—after a while, she refused to visit my family.

the new grandfather's curse is not exactly a curse
she'll ruin your life is a knot
an erroneous racist tangle of poorly thought thought
A.'s mother will not let his knot curse their lives
it goes underground
what A. understood of that day is now completely unknown

A.'s mother's father and my father too   the new grandfather
was known for his firm fixed opinions
his commonplace unfounded intolerance
sparing no   one except maybe himself   or maybe not

I was watering the potted begonias that sat on the west-facing sill
when the phone rang
and through the window the day blazed with the snow-capped mountain range to
the north

do you know what he said
how could I know
she'll ruin your life is what he said
no   meaning how could he
yes   my life   my sister said

he doesn't know what he's talking about
what does he know about your life   I said   he never did

his callous his everyday intolerant discrimination

he will die in a year   but his words   his words will not
bigotry   always cruel   unfounded   always reluctant to perish
with or without the bigoted one

Not that she was a stranger to problems but
she had not been a mother before
arduous mothering being differently problematical
attachment for instance   being so close
being so heart-hurtable   and everyday tested

A. it can be no surprise
needed special assistance in school

and so it began
the public
the systems   the systems
that do not love her
and never have

the whole family
becoming so public

even when privacy
was so desperately prized

The No-Longer-New Mother (a.k.a. my little sister)

Another problem with racism, one of those everyday problems, is that when the third-grade teacher tells me A. is disruptive in class, and then tells me that A. needs to be broken and that she, the teacher, close to retirement and who never did like A., that she can break her. Break her! The problem then is that I don't know whether this teacherly hostility is because A. is really so disruptive in class or whether it's because A. is Black. Or because the teacher is about to retire. She said, "I can break her." Her precise words. I hardly knew what to say.

Interesting that the word "profiling" is used in policing and in the criminal justice systems but not in the educational and medical systems where it also belongs.

there were Psych Ed tests
batteries (sic)
of psychological tests
that finally
recommended

1. teaching assistance

2. medication

3. one-to-one in the classroom

Later much later on the phone my sister tells me when I ask

What did I feel when I tore up those Psych. Ed. documents? Sorrow, yes, plain, flat sorrow for how much A. had tried, but it hadn't clicked into place.

And anger for the systems that hurt her beyond what any little girl could barely endure. And yet there she had been, trying her best. Anger for how the assessments were written, like a business report, with no sense that a real live concerned family member would read them, but my overwhelming emotion was pissed off. The thoughtlessness. How the assessments were drafted.

Sad too for her aloneness in the world, for having to have lived through things that led to her being tested. If those things hadn't happened, her brain, her mind would have been hugely happy, gigantically successful, enormously full of life and positive, hopeful expectations.

Lonely for me, as well, for sitting through all those interviews and meetings with 'the team': school psychologists, social workers, and special ed teachers, and me, always a place set for me at the very end of the meeting table. Lonely reading their assessments and I remember how I had tried to think of the best way forward.

But mostly, as I said, really pissed off. The assessments all began with a 'social history.' The codes here: that she was Black, that she was adopted, that she was being brought up by a single mother, these stereotypes for failure, for let's just give up on her. And every single assessment made sloppy errors in the social history, e.g., where she was born, date of birth. No assessment ever spoke of what she was like as a real living person.

And of course, they always had all the power and the decision making.

Oh, and I almost forgot to mention. After the assessment news, having to go home and be cheerful, cheery, with my kids when I felt so deflated for them. They both had assessments with no apparent answers or decent educational or emotional support in sight. Holding it all in from them, protecting them from feelings of not making it, not cutting it, not fitting in. Trying to spin these situations in a sort of positive way. The lack of respect within the assessments, the humiliation, the disruption.

Last night I had a dream that my house was on fire and the fire station didn't answer the phone. I walked over there and they told me to go to another station across town. I walked for two days to get there. When I got there, they told me to go back home.

attachment is a fixed finite construction
what is there in this story that could have been safely uncoupled
the Rideau Canal   the snow   traffic flow   the kitchen counter
a different dog falling through mid-canal

Salvador Dalí's clock drapes the new edge of history
a new age   not making a sound when A.'s story
could not garner the right kind of attention   history's struck non-linear clock

we know this: the mind cannot separate
the emotional cortex
                                        from what is considered the logical one

what is known is only the tip
what A. experienced outside the house
in the streets   in school corridors   on the bus
lay underneath

There will come a time when A. is ten when Mrs. Smiley
A.'s long-standing kindly teaching assistant
will phone the new mother at her government office to ask the new mother
to come to the school to persuade A. to resurface from under her desk

And the new mother will go to the school
will coax A. out from under the desk

                                        the only one able

you'll never guess what happened today
and no   I never could
yes   under the desk   it took twenty minutes   I took her home
we sat at the table and ate chocolate cookies
I did not go back to the office

Mrs. Smiley for years sent Christmas cards
and then one day   a decade after A. had died   out of the blue
she called A.'s mother
to say   *Hello I've been thinking of A.*

who has not been thinking of A.
her laugh   her incredible smile

A.'s Teaching Assistant (Jean Smiley)

Spirited is the word I use for her. As in lively. As in haunted. Hunted. Oh my, she was fast. She could take care of herself. Prescient too. After I gave her my home phone number, forbidden of course by the Ottawa School Board, she became more amenable. That's how she knew I cared about her. Never hid under her desk again.

I never learned how many

                classroom disruptions

                                disappearances from home

wrists slashings

                razors found in her drawers

hospital visits

            hospital stays

loud nights and sleepless

        loud mornings and aching fatigue

        how much how many

how deep bleak

how much A. how much the family

when A. was eleven almost twelve she slipped the known limits of her navigational self

slipped out of the day having fallen

                    into a coma

the hospital called A.'s mother

in her government office A. was deep in a coma after a fall very deep

beyond the rim of the world

that fearless that fast she was running

was there someone something in dogged pursuit

from whom was she running what where was she running to

when my sister called me *A.'s in the hospital*

              she's in a coma

she left me a message on my machine

I couldn't tell she was crying

I didn't know then how much attention

then at that time I needed to pay

I thought she'll recover she's young

my sister called me again

                why haven't you called me back

she's been in a coma since Tuesday
today is Thursday
I've been crying the whole time

in any moment   all that is not known   in any moment
between any two people   two lives
I was wrapped in my own

a coma was something else I couldn't fix

A.'s Mother

Of course, yes, there were accidents. So much was frightening. So much official-dom, each piece of paper, so much tension, so many unknowns and the possibility always of everything falling apart. From the state Government in Brazil and their courts, from the adoption agency, from the Federal Government Adoption Desk in Canada, and from the Children's Aid Society and Immigration Canada and from the School Board.

I was really happy when she became a citizen. Her sister's adoption application was even more fraught, the possibility of it never coming through which would have been terrible, completely unbearable.

The Mother

When A. arrived, I didn't even know how to manage her hair. I say manage, but what I mean is, I couldn't brush it or even wash it well enough. Look at my hair, look at hers.

3.

Twelve Being a Negative Number

The giddy soul trying to get out from the top of the head
Mark Doty

Kuska (Dog Number 2)

Oh yes A. was fast almost as fast as I am and I'm a bona fide Weimaraner fastest dog in the world after the Greyhound of course and the German Shepherd, maybe even the Vizsla. But I am very fast. A. was very fast too. She wasn't afraid hardly of anything at all. She held me when the vet gave me the needle. Years ago. I'm big, but she held me in her lap on the vet's floor. She was big enough. She was my best friend; I think I was her best friend too.

Tidy (Dog Number 3)

A. always sat me up in her lap like I was a Dachshund-ish queen. In her wheelchair. She had a big lap in that chair. And a big laugh to match. Sometimes she'd sing me "You Ain't Nothin but a Hound Dog," sounding more Satchmo than Elvis.

Poppy (Dog Number 1)

I remember the day A. arrived. She got into the car, took one look at me, slid over, and sat scrunched up against the car door all the way home. I slid away from the skirt of her big purple coat. I kept my eyes closed, my head down. Later I had her eating out of my paws.

later · more than two decades later   the teen years and somehow
graduations
basketball and a friend   even a boyfriend
and the plans for her life
beginning to collide

the plans   the aspirations
the immense power of hope
time flipping by like the calendar pages in an old Hollywood movie
she was depressed
she had spent months
on juvenile wards
months
and the third dog was still alive

even then she was suicidal

The Mother

Once, at least once, I heard yelling outside and when I looked out the window, there was A. surrounded by three neighbours, adults, out there on the street where she was just bouncing a basketball. It was late afternoon. She was fourteen. They were yelling for her to stop stop that infernal … Were they being racist? I called her in.

The scent of snow this night
still smells something like lemons
clotted maybe with car fumes
hot oil   pepperoni   the old pizza parlour there on the corner

midnight or half-past midnight   A.'s pretty sure
midwinter   but ever since she lost her wristwatch
or did she give it away
she's thirty-three years old and she needs
to be back at the facility for midnight curfew   okay she's late
snow drumming down cold as steel bullets
sharp cymbals and stars
Bank Street already devoid
when
her wheelchair   yes   she now uses a wheelchair   so much has happened
and winters are worst
such a slow mode for her who has always been fast
suddenly
the wheels catch   become stuck   the wheels
wedged   jammed in the rutted razor-sharp ice
the frozen street hodgepodged   tire-marked
footprinted with rime
the wheelchair battery now running low
mid-street   then the battery running out altogether

she's stuck in the middle   almost middle
a pickup honks as it swerves to the right
and her heart   and the lights
when she remembers the new government policy
her mother told her   hammer heart
that small drum inside
the new Ministry directive   directing
wheelchair clients   must obtain three estimates
three repair quotes   before calling
before contracting the services
of a wheelchair technician

she thinks of her mother   she always thinks of her mother

past midnight
and keeping in mind the award-winning Ottawa cold
the frost freezing   her ears   the tips stinging
without her new tricoloured hat
where did her hat go   and her mitts
her cigarettes   opening her coat   fishing inside the inner pocket
she finds only one
but where is her lighter
the traffic light shines red a half block away
she's under a streetlight   its sodium haunt
and here come four men   past midnight   weaving wild over the road
four men who only know how to laugh   how to shove and guffaw

she has given away her mauve coloured mitts
why   her mother will ask her   just because
and she is not in the mood
to obtain the three requisite quotes
she has the number of only one

the four men have been drinking   laughing now overloud
they almost drown out the sound of her heart
she is stuck

           O

           n the ic

           e dotted street mid r

           oad bea

           ds of sw

           eat on

           he

           r bare brow

in the ruts
of the ice

finding her cell   and of course
she calls her mother   who will

her mother will answer the phone
never mind the rule   only five-calls-a-day

at night her mother always answers the phone

trapped in the middle almost the middle
immovable in her black battery-operated
her chair   her life
stuck on the road where the cars might
and her mother

I know I know
she can hear the downturn of her mother's mouth
the battery and I don't have a hat

her mother too
stuck   taking the call   past midnight   the stuck clock of history
how life can grind to a point
but the four men are slowing   stopping   are saying
do you need   do you want us to
and they carry her
                        tilting   listing a bit to the left
                        in her unwieldy chair over the impossible ice
crunching onto the sidewalk also slick   placing her down

and now she can laugh too
fear having massed   pent up   passed
wouldn't you
her mother still on the phone   saying
which corner
where the old pizza parlour   you know the one
and can you bring me a pack of cigarettes
and my lighter   I left my lighter on the hall table

smiling   relieved when her mother arrives in the car
maybe anger is almost like laughter
maybe fear is almost like grief

Kenny (one of the men who helped A. to the sidewalk)

I'd seen her before, one day in October she was on Bank Street and I saw her giving away cigarettes. Maybe she was quitting. She gave one to me. So I said to my buddy, Dave, I said, she needs help. I wasn't completely smashed, just trying to keep warm. Heavy as an old sofa, that chair, and she was heavy too. Dave almost fell, but we made it across. I don't think she expected us to be, like, decent, you know? It still makes me feel pretty good. What can I say? You don't get many chances like that.

this is not strictly biographical   certainly not linear
                                   not the line of a life lived unimpeded
not of A.'s life   nor her mother's   nor her first mother's

not every life is an uninterrupted unbroken straight line
of what we call progress
not everything has always been planned
                      not all parts of A.'s life are known
                                                or will ever be known

when she began to show signs   but when did she not show any signs
nor are all the signs fully recorded
not all the details are wholly correct
not the entire range of A.'s numberless medications
over the years   each endless doctor
dosages in some cases yes may be known
but not all   in this not-so-straight line of a life

her mother kept her own lists
Ramipril (white/red capsule) / blood pressure
Avandia (pink five-sided tablet) / diabetes
Diltiazem (grey light blue capsule) / blood pressure
Trazodone (white round tablet) / sleep
Glyburide (white oblong tablet) / diabetes
Epival (peach oval tablet) / mood stabilizer
Metformin (white round tablet) / diabetes
Furosemide (yellow round tablet) / water retention
Atorvastatin (white oval tablet) / cholesterol
Metoprolol (pink oblong tablet) / blood pressure
Loxapine (yellow round tablet) / anti-psychotic
Sennosides (blue or brown tablet) / laxative
Acetaminophen / Tylenol (white round tablet) / pain
Sertraline (yellow capsule) / not noted
Olanzapine / Zydis (yellow wafer) / anti-psychotic
Lactulose (yellow liquid) / laxative

not known either is the number or quality of incidental encounters or
accidents or deliberations
inside or outside the house

The Mother

When she was eleven or maybe she was already twelve, she started leaving me notes. She never wanted to turn twelve. How to stop time? Leaving the notes on the kitchen table or on the counter, sometimes on the navy-blue dresser across from my bed. Little square pieces of paper written in her looping hand. Notes of distress. I saved every one.

Nothing helps I'm feeling
alot of pain meaning emotional
pain its really hard to talk
about it.

She placed her pain on the page

unlined scraps of pink paper
where it lay
in a ravel   entangled
a sorrow
a small square of paper
same words
articulate as any theorem
over and over
again
no need for the fine points

Two other things happen. Three, in fact, in the tradition of fables and lyric poems, magical spells. Maybe more, but these are the ones her mother reported to me.

1. A. left the house in the dark at 9 p.m. and did not return. 1990. She was twelve. She had never wanted to turn the corner to twelve. Turn twelve and things turn momentous. Her mother left the house at 11 p.m. to find her, driving the Queensway looking, looking, her head swivelling side to side as she drove under the high-up sodium lights as if in a fairy tale trance. October, cold rain beginning to fall and at midnight turning lightly to snow. Did she find her that time or had she returned home on her own? It would happen again. And again.

My sister called me later:

> have you seen the movie Iris about Iris Murdoch   how her husband   the way her husband had to get in the car at night and drive around trying to find her when she left the house in a fog.
>
> I couldn't watch that part of the movie   that was me driving all over Ottawa over and over again.

2. A. sat in the basement on the cold cement floor. 1992. Breaking glass, an old empty jar. Unbiddable. She did not write on the walls. She was fifteen years old. Maybe performing an argument against the unbearable weight of world history or her own history or the weight of real time, the numberless wrongs, the number of apologies needed to right the record. Maybe she was trying to break the cycle of hurt, the sound of glass crashing onto the floor, pieces of stars, the moon weeping, shedding shrill tears. She needed a shard sharp enough to break the soft inner skin of her lower left wrist just up from the heel of her thumb. A certain heart-breaking unspeakable glass-shattering racket high-pitched becoming the sound of outer-space inner-space carillon bells.

I ask my sister again:

> do you think a counsellor might help? It's too much to
> handle on your own. The head banging, the breakage,
> the loud waking at night.

But no, nothing like that ever worked.

A. left the psych hospital youth ward one afternoon where she'd stayed for five months and would stay for two more. The year of the infamous Ottawa ice storm, 1997, that left trees shining like rock candy, the limbs cracking with ice as if varnished, broken and bent. City crews chain-sawing the trees in the aftermath, clearing the piled up splintered wood, the impossible tangles of branches felled by the weight of the cold. Whining chainsaw sounds of constructive destruction.

A. left the hospital midday, it had stopped snowing, and found a city crew down by the Ottawa River, three men, axes and saws, beside a large City truck. A. asked politely. She was uneasy and she asked as politely as she could ask. Please, she said, can I borrow a chainsaw? Not for long, she promised. Just for herself. It would not take her long.

what does pain sound like

               emotional pain

like a spoon ribbing thick metal bars
or a gale from the north

the sound of fish knives after the fish
breath caught in rocks   winter-fouled ice
starlings kept in a cage

like static at the end of the line
or like nothing   like no one there at the other end of the phone
nothing   no one at all

alterity
she was in the achingly odd state
of being painfully unalike

How much light-hearted does a heavy heart need
and what kind
bemusement of course
irony
a half-wink
a smile
chuckles
a joke
funny stories over the phone
so hilarious you cannot stop crying

Here's another thing I heard happened. Over the phone. A lot of history has happened over the phone.

It's a long story. In fact, two. This is the first. A. was twenty-eight, living with her boyfriend at the time. Pierre. She became depressed, suicidal. It was 2004. She took a taxi to the ER at the General and the ER took too long. It was a Saturday. A lot of other people must have been depressed that winter weekend. After an hour, A. needed a smoke. She had to wait until the ER nurse could find an escort, an orderly, to take her outside. Hospital protocol. So that A. could smoke on the car ramp just outside the Emergency Room. She was suicidal which was why she went to the hospital in the first place. She smoked her cigarette and then went back inside where she once again waited in the crowded ER. And then she waited some more. Finally, she needed another cigarette. This time the nurse said, sure, go have a smoke. But this time the nurse omitted the escort.

A. jumped from the parking ramp two stories above the driveway before she even lit up. Two storeys down. Damaged her heart her lungs her liver her kidneys her back and her neck her head her brain her wrist her dental formula and her beautiful smile. The minerals of her mouth her shining teeth her jawbone. The breakdown of her fine jawbone. Two storeys onto the ramp. Her whole mouth over time will break down. Her whole life moment by moment. What else is there but time. She went home three weeks later in a lavish neck brace.

This is all going too fast, yes, it all went too fast; no one could stop the straight line of time.

I flew to Ottawa. The neck brace was awkward, but A. was safe. Her mother, all of us, had wanted her, most of all, to be safe. For months before the jump, A. had been hard to track. She lived in her own small apartment and she called her mother when she needed money or a carton of cigarettes. She was 29. She moved fast. It was always so hard to keep her sufficiently safe.

And then this happened. Which is the second story. All this time she'd been living with her boyfriend, Pierre. They lived together in A.'s apartment on the fourth floor, but because of her jump from the car ramp, A. no longer trusted herself not to jump again, so she decided to stay with two friends on the building's first floor. For three months. The boyfriend stayed alone in her fourth-floor apartment. He was a hoarder, he brought home all sorts of junk. The apartment got jammed up with junk. You could hardly walk through the hallways. After three months, A. agreed to return to her own apartment on the fourth floor where he had continued to stay. She became increasingly depressed. He seemed nice enough, but he wasn't. Not nearly enough.

One day in February, a few weeks after she'd moved back into her own apartment, she tried to run away from him, maybe he was threatening her, out onto the small apartment balcony, snow heaping there. She was almost never afraid. But this time. This time she jumped. To get away. Maybe. Four storeys down onto the sidewalk, onto the frozen cement. 2006. Four stories down. Damaged her feet her legs her spine her back her bladder pelvis hips her hip bones and her hip joints. This time she spent five weeks in hospital. Her damaged kidney was left in her body. The doctors decided not to repair her two broken hips nor did they set her pelvis nor her feet, nor her spine. Her spine was severed, they said, they said it could not be fixed. Her mother persisted, at least her hips, she had begged. They said A. would never have feeling below her waist ever again. But they were wrong.

They had their own spurious reasons:

1. A. was a woman.
2. She was heavy.
3. She had made a suicide attempt (in fact, two).
4. She had almost no money.
5. She was heavy.
6. She was a heavy Black woman with mental illness with almost no money who had made two suicide attempts. With no clear diagnosis.
7. Her spine was severed (in fact, it was crushed).
8. She was fearless. And a little bit loud.
9. She was Black.

The Mother

I know this: if A. had had a blond ponytail, her spine would have been repaired. Nothing I said to those doctors, begged them, begged them, made one wit of difference.

This unfortunate unfounded medical decision resulted in continuous pain. More pain than A. had already known. She required constant pain medication. She used a wheelchair every day. She was catheterized. She became diabetic. She suffered pressure sores. She was slowed down. She became completely dependent.

though she smiled often
even laughed   loved to laugh
hugged   shouted out   ecstatic at times
sang   would have danced

maybe anger is almost like fear
maybe fear is almost like hurt

for sure she'd been hurt

the second time she jumped was February
first time was mid-November   those two short winter months
ice months and snow

all that year   all the days in between   the days following too
between sores and catheters and a crushed spine
half a lung

like Gandhi she gives things away
her wool hat   her fleece gloves   her scarf   a bracelet
the green earrings I gave her the summer before
a five-dollar bill
sometimes even her last cigarette

A. can hear birds speak
sometimes she sees them flitting in thickets   twitching
from the side of her eye   once I might have seen one myself
did you see it she asks me   and maybe I did
sometimes she sings   a torch angel in a motorized chair
"What a Wonderful World"

I can't tell you exactly what happened to my sister that year
really happened   the void there   the bedridden despair
the days in between   the days following too

Rohitassa was a Buddhist deva, a seer, a powerful sky-walker whose speed was fast as an arrow, whose stride stretched as far as the east sea is from the west. And endowed with such speed, such a stride, Rohitassa desired to journey to the end of the cosmos. And with a one-hundred-year span of life, he decided to spend one hundred years travelling—and apart from time spent eating, drinking, chewing and tasting, urinating and defecating and sleeping, to fight off weariness, to never stop moving.

And he never stopped moving, but without reaching the end of the cosmos, still travelling, still moving fast, he died on the way.

I tell you, said the Buddha: It is not possible by travelling to know or see or reach a far end of the cosmos where one does not take birth, age, die, pass away or reappear. But at the same time, I tell you that there is no making an end of suffering and stress without reaching the end of the cosmos. Yet it is just within this fathom-long body with its perception and intellect that I declare that there is the cosmos, the origination of the cosmos, the cessation of the cosmos and the path of practice leading to the cessation of the cosmos.

A.'s life racing, all the while I'm hoping she'll approach a turn in the road, a corner, a hill, a staircase, something that might change her direction, her cosmic velocity. In the multiplicity of history, even in her wheelchair, looking for that loophole. Some form of release. I guarantee: inside, she never stopped moving. For sure she had been pursued. For sure she'd been hurt.

4.

Worn Down and Weeping

There are no straight lines in nature
Yusuf Saadi

This is another thing about her mother but also about A.:

A. was twenty-six when her mother travelled to Sierra Leone, staying there for two months to research war-affected girls. There were so many. She stayed in Freetown with five nuns in a small convent house in the city. There were no hotels or vacation rentals or B & Bs, and the five nuns had remained in Sierra Leone throughout the whole civil/uncivil war in the 90s. No one who could have left Sierra Leone stayed. A trauma-sick city in a trauma-thick country.

At the end of Fort Street, an ancient building, some sort of warehouse, overlooked the salt water. An ominous stone remainder/reminder, now serving as an elementary school, the nuns told her when she returned that afternoon. They told her this was the building where slave traders kept captured slaves until the slave ships came to take them away. To Brazil. Her daughters' ancestors had been imprisoned there in that very building on that very street in Freetown. This much, A.'s mother knew in her heart to be true.

The Mother

In Freetown so many young people had no hands. Their arms stopped at their wrists. In the war, the soldiers, or maybe the rebel—the sides were often unclear—hacked off the hands of young people. They were mostly all children. Girls too. Some had no feet. In this way these children were prevented from fighting on the wrong side, whatever the wrong side happened to be. Something about diamonds, engagement rings, wedding rings, something romantic—bloody romantic.

I must ask you, A., even though you can no longer say: What made you think twelve was a perilous age, so unsafe you declined that numerical corner? And yet... From then on, every year becoming more risky. The trespass of time pushing hard from behind. December 8th arrived overnight in 1988, and later that day cake was sliced and the song sung.

You never feared eleven. Why twelve?

Was it the one dozen apostles? Or the twelve sons of Jacob forming the twelve tribes of Israel? Judas? Or because the twelve gates of the kingdom are guarded by the twelve angels? Months of the year? Constellations of the zodiac? Puberty?

Twelve, they say is sublime, an abundant number. Was that the reason? They say the Virgin Mary stayed in the temple 12 years. Jesus was 12 when he questioned the scholars. Twelve legions of angels. Types of fruit on the tree?

Dangerous? A dozen eggs, but ten fingers, ten toes, thirty-two teeth by the time you're thirteen. Two-hundred-thirty bones in the body. The glass darkly. Catastrophizing the whole decade and decades to come. And yet you refused fear, none, never, not one nano of fear. Very little.

Twelve arrived, settled in and yes things got more serious. I say serious but that's not the word. It was much more frightening than that.

Let the wind keep her aloft. Let it propel her safely through time.

You lived in a home-studied house while the schoolyard the streets of the city
the parks were not vetted at all who did you have who could warn you of this
this place this white town sometimes snow on the ground and you on the move
on your own on the streets even with very high doses of slow-you-down drugs
ball-bearinged skates as though you were a deva with skate-keys and a voice like
a heart already burning striding to the end of the world dying before you could
circuit the stars

after the seventh hospitalization she cannot go home
at age twenty-one A. cannot go home
everyone at home is completely worn out
everyone at home is in bed and crying all day
her mother my sister her sister so much had gone wrong
worn down to the ground worn down and weeping
neither mother nor sister could leave the house on most days
those frantic years they could not leave their beds
worn prone for the day and for the night tissues all-day pyjamas
all the love in the world unstoppable

after breaking the window too much was at risk
the police had attended
therefore jail and one month of solitary confinement isolation

seven months on a ward
everything too fast and not fast enough
begging to be allowed to come home to the worn-down family and family home

then the Y apartments social housing shelters group homes facility care hospital wards

everything too painful and the caring systems not caring enough
all the love in the world and weeping everyone weeping

Here's another story I hear happened time to time—around 2007—over the phone.

Whenever A. went to Rockin' Johnny's diner situated in the elbow of Westgate Mall near the house on Dovercourt and close to the Royal Ottawa, her mother tugging open Rockin' Johnny's glass door, standing aside to let A. wheel herself in from the cold, all the waiters there knowing her, shouting out welcomes, moving chairs, making room for her wheelchair, making a lot of noise for her, and A. would shout *fries* and they'd laugh and shout back, *burger with cheese. And Pepsi,* she'd shout back, yes, always Pepsi with ice. As if a feast for a visiting royal.

She and her mother, who was a vegetarian, who ate only the well-salted fries, they both would eat the fries, and A. would eat the burger with cheese. Pepsi with ice. A feast. She'd slip a coin into the jukebox and the diner would fill up with her favourite, "What a Wonderful World." And she'd sing along.

Everyone was still alive then, except the great-grandfather who'd died decades before and the woman's father, my father too, A.'s grandfather, who'd predicted familial ruination and Gordian knots. And the woman's mother who died two years before A. arrived. Everyone else then was still alive.

5.

She Knew What She Knew
before It Was Known

You can endure almost anything as long as you can sing about it.

James Wright

on the way back to the hospital   ten admissions and she is now thirty-five
the Royal Ottawa   cement walls and glass
after dinner   shrimp with rice and later the cheesecake
loving the cheesecake topped with red berries and nuts
we walk A. back to the ward   twenty minutes away
A. saying goodbye to her old house   wheeling down the old road dead-ended on the
east end
she knows the road well   she grew up here
her old bike and her ball-bearing skates
then crossing the major arterial street   four lanes across
taking then the path through the small urban woods
twenty minutes from the house to the ward where she lives
the scent of damp earth and the big leaf maple leaves
early fall and the walk   root systems and cigarette butts
twenty minutes of twilight   two streetlamps lighting the path through the woods
walking back to the ward where she   barely lighting the woods
where she lives   has lived for six months
the earthen path darkening   she is leading the way
and the dog with very short legs trying to keep up to the wheels
her mother and me   trying to
keeping up some small conversation
so we didn't have to
and she begins singing
and all we can do   is listen
that evening the Ottawa Propeller Dance Company   springtime 2011
Twenty performers choreographed up there on the stage
varieties of dance   dancers   walkers and wheelchairs
some performers just standing on stage looking out
into the blinding mainstream
the house lights   what a wonderful world

                          and then

                          the spotlight finds A. mid-stage in her
                    wheelchair
she has already started to sing   not missing a beat
the audience   we are bending   leaning into her voice   deep   leaning into the sound

it could almost reflect the night sky on the edge of a forest
daubed with deep purple ink
falling under her thrall   heads tilting up   "What a Wonderful World"
the other performers   stilled as small rabbits

and I think to myself   and I think to myself

I keep following A. her movements   over the phone every week   twice a week
for years every week   landline black on the wall
new phone beige on the shelf   cell phone grey in the hand
through myriad snags   around corners   a bend in the road
following loosely behind
trepidations   confusions   one hitch to the next
very little of ease leading in any direction

A. spends the last half of her life mainly in hospital beds
some nurses love her   others do not   the doctors are never there

her mother can hardly bear to open the heavy glass doors
or walk through the lobbies to the silver-doored lifts
it all takes one thousand years

one spring I arrive with my sister into the Royal Ottawa parking lot
and from across the broad stretch of parked cars
I hear her voice   A.'s booming bright voice
TIA TIA   that's my aunt   she shouts into the small crowd around her
my aunt   my aunt   she's here to visit me
A. is bouncing in her black chair   *Tia Tia*
where she sits on the hospital's aproned cement   ebullient   look at her
she is tethered yes to this hospital but in a way that seems
not to diminish her spirit   *TIA TIA*   untethering herself   and I shout to her
across the tops of the cars to where she sits
in front of the hospital doors with maybe ten others   smoking   all smoking
I close the car door   feeling welcome   very welcome
aiming straight for a hug

how A. knew what she knew   how darkness survives also beyond the locked closet
we say mental illness   we say medication
psychiatric institution facility care
racism   we say a young woman at large in the world
whose heart is a torch

sorrow   how many years   deracination   these Americas   this world
pain   unseen even in the bright light of midday

The Mother Writes to the Director of A.'s Last Care Facility

Dear Mr. Last,
December 13, 2012

Thank you for your email yesterday in reply to my urgent emails (and letter) of December 6th and 7th which concern my daughter A.'s sudden eviction/transfer from your facility last week.

You say in your reply that she "was not evicted," that she was "transferred to a hospital with the resources and ability to manage her care. A. was discharged from the facility because we cannot, and never will be able, to provide the care she requires." Your distinction between "evicted" and "transferred" would seem, under these circumstances (i.e., that her room has been cleared of her belongs; that I was called and told she was being evicted—that term was in fact used—and that you seem to be refusing to have her back) to be a matter of semantics, which obscures the real issue: that A. is in hospital for treatment, not for housing, and despite your opinion that she has been transferred "to a hospital with the resources and ability to provide the care she needs," no hospital can offer continuing housing. Nonetheless, you seem to be suggesting that the hospital may in effect be her housing alternative. I'm sure you understand, as I do, that acute-care hospitalization cannot be a housing option for anyone. And facility staff have not mentioned other options for her placement.

Further, the facility has cared for A.'s needs for over two years without any discussion of her having to leave for any reason, medical or psychiatric. And although she has been hospitalized in the past two years, the facility has never cleared her room in the past, nor requested her belongings be picked up. As well, she has had ACT team services in addition to her care at the facility. The ACT team activation worker and psychiatrist have managed her social, recreational and psychiatric needs for the past two years while she has been living at the facility and have been available to consult with your staff. I believe that the facility continues to have responsibility for providing accommodation and care for my daughter, that her belongings should not be removed from her room and that her room should remain hers until she can be safely housed and cared for in another facility in an ongoing way.

Sincerely,

The Mother

Not that she hadn't written letters before   many   and attended official meetings
and unofficial   spoken to nurses teachers police doctors dentists counsellors
neighbours facility managers made phone calls purchased clothes to fit   hats mitts
boots   bought cigarettes   bought sandwiches hamburgers fries   Pepsi with ice

they think I'm overinvolved   she tells me over the phone
it's Saturday afternoon
there are three bags of groceries on my kitchen counter
and outside the rain can't stop falling

they think I'm a complainer   a complainer!!
which means
they can stop paying attention to me
I'm only the mother

there is so much to complain about
and she is only the mother

6.

No Kind of Ending

this hunger entering our / loneliness like birds
Lucille Clifton

the better part of her last year   A.   in hospital wheeling along corridors in a cumbersome over-large chair   she is now thirty-six and fully familiar with hospital wards hospital food hospital beds nurses doctors cleaners security cameras security personnel routines patients smoking regulations elevators hallways walls green walls of dissonance white doors of boredom bulletin boards catheters needles paper-cup meds in the morning lunchtime and just before bed.

six seven eight admissions maybe ten   each one lasting three months or twelve sometimes   at least once   they strap her to her hospital bed   for her own good

then November 16   it happens this fast   one pill   a certain psychotropic prescription   the dosage too high   already in hospital for almost eight months   when A.'s heart   which had time to time in the past year paused   pausing time to time on a day pass   because of that particular pill   all of a sudden finally stopped   and did not start again.

3 a.m. on the psych ward   resuscitation attempts   wires   tubes   defibrillator pads

her mother   my sister   is called   her phone rings three times   3 a.m. and she leaps out of bed into the dark

I imagine the phone call   I imagine the dark   I imagine her pulling on her socks boots   her sweater   her coat   I am on the other side of the country and there is nothing to do but to cry

when she arrives at the hospital   3:20 a.m.   when she enters A.'s room   A. is still in the bed with tubes criss-crossing her chest and into her nose   but A. is no longer there.

November 16   one pill   a new pill on her long list of pills
causing her heart
to pause
stop
her heart   her big risk-taking raucous warm ardent
sing-songing ecstatic loud heart   her generous heart
to stop
and the nurses on their night rounds
2:30 a.m.   the phone call   my sister   the no-longer-new mother

when she arrives   she walks the 3:20 half-lit hospital halls
enters the room   the bright lights there and A. flat on the bed
criss-crossed with tubing and wires
is already gone

on the Queensway   the mother   well-seasoned and
on the way home   snow
smelling now of confusion   yes
and of gloom   snow
                                        is beginning to fall
fat flakes   falling fast in the headlights
                                        falling apart   the continuous unfolding
deep time
the times she drove the Queensway looking looking
for A.

the times she drove A. back
home
to her first apartment
to the shelter
to the hospital
the drive into the city when A. first arrived in the city
that early April in '85 when the snow

but now A. is gone

hold her hand   keep her safe   bring her home

this is the time they have had together   A. and her mother
they both wanted more
why not   as if they were not already cleaved
where are those corners   the gaps
and yet   at which point could this story have saved itself
at which point would time have had stand still   pivot
wrenching clocks   alter its inflexible course   its route
round that corner   expand   change its mind
tick tock in another direction   backwards   blow-back from the winds of the past
not looking behind
looking into a new improved future   perfect   beginning again
in the back seat of the apple red car
snow falling that day and the sudden burst
of the subsequent sun   three hundred years ago

how much snow that night November 16
the road to the hospital weeping with salt
the falling snow like whitened bone lace
furling unfurling   the mother's mind
this witness

who then wouldn't choose a new story
how many children   mothers and mothers
the Angel of History
this child among many

to counter the counter where small squares of paper
notes written over with pain

but none of us able to change it
not me or my sister or A. or her sister
not the nurses or doctors not the counsellors or teachers
not the care workers or pharmacists or friends

not the birds or the books we all read
none of us could really fix anything of any importance
none of us could revise one minute of time

the power over is history

not a singular story but a collective   all things being related
burdens   layers of this filtered-unfiltered account
her spirit her smile
she never stops singing   her voice will ripen with time

what if no child were ever born in the trash
even the notion the metaphor   completely outrageous

or kept in a locked closet

we've been told 74 million meadow larks
have disappeared in one decade
some stories turn over too fast

in the framed photograph on the mantle
which stays for all time on that north-facing shelf
the birds there never leave A.'s two open hands
her two arms sparrowed and juncoed   one robin
its wingspan having just landed feathers fanned
a small finch a chickadee black-capped they do not leave
do not disappear   the colours in the photograph
are always red blue and silver
her sports jacket bright satin white
red stripes down the two outer sleeves autumn
in a clear wooded space no longer April but still almost green

the Experimental Farm where the photo was taken
is bright with bright yellow brush
where A. worked one summer
in one of the barns devoted to cows

in the picture she has allowed four or five songbirds
mercy they alight
they never leave her two arms her two hands
everything still and watching her eyes on the robin

this story has no way of stopping
even after the end
the ashes are still on the mantle

she is not the only one
not the story   nor the hum of the story
not the hum but the electrical charge

those songbirds with their fine fanning wings
a silent ovation
she is being transfigured   she is a tree with branches and leaves
those birds
they will not fly away
they never leave her two shining arms

Acknowledgements and Notes

Huge and humble thanks to Donna, my sister and friend, for including me in her life and for allowing me to write about this part of her life and of the life of her older daughter, A., and for sharing documents and pictures, for sharing her life. I owe her so much. She has written a compelling memoir, *Falling Together*, about her life with A., and I heartily recommend it.

Thanks, as well, to her younger daughter, my niece, Renata, for who she is and for being brilliant and valiant.

Thanks to my son, Peter Paré, for helping me to properly first redact and then insert the documents that appear in this book and for helping me tighten the lined poems on pages 28 and 103.

Thanks to the members of my two writing groups for their clear, useful, always supportive feedback.

Thanks, too, to John Barton, poet and friend, for his careful and valuable early reading of this manuscript.

As well, many thanks to Sadiqa de Meijer for her valuable, sensitive early reading of this manuscript.

Thanks to Hoa Nguyen, poet and teacher, who led me to C.D. Wright's *One with Others*, to which I owe the (somewhat altered) formatting and style of this book, and to C.D. Wright for her wonderful book in the first place.

Thanks to Alex Gallagher and Pat Hurdle for research regarding 1985 aircraft.

Thanks to David Pimm for research regarding the number twelve.

Information on Duplessis Children was written by Jaela Bernstien at the CBC and was found on Wikipedia.

The story of Rohitassa, adapted on page 120, is a classical Buddhist story in the Theravādin tradition.

The reference to the Angel of History on page 47 and 137 is from Walter Benjamin.

Lucille Clifton, excerpts from "blake," "[the angels have no wings]," and "in the same week" from *The Collected Poems of Lucille Clifton*. Copyright © 1996, 2004 by Lucille Clifton. Reprinted with the permission of The Permissions Company, LLC on behalf of BOA Editions Ltd., boaeditions.org.

So much appreciation to Susan Olding, whose crucial and careful edits allowed this manuscript to become its best self.

Massive thanks to Vici Johnstone, Sarah Corsie and Malaika Aleba, the amazing team at Caitlin Press, for their care and efforts on behalf of this collection. They are simply fantastic.

Finally, heartfelt thanks to Chris Fox, my wife and companion for over forty-three years, first reader, first editor, tech support and owner of a wide-ranging reference library, for her perpetual and loving support.

ABOUT THE AUTHOR

Arleen Paré is a writer with eight collections of poetry, based in Victoria, BC. She has been short-listed for the Dorothy Livesay BC Book Award for Poetry and has twice won the American Golden Crown Award for Lesbian Poetry. She has also won the Victoria Butler Book Prize, a CBC Bookie Award, a bpNichol Chapbook Award and a Governor General's Award for Poetry.

This book is set in Arno Pro, a font designed by Robert Slimbach.
The text was typeset by Vici Johnstone of
Caitlin Press, Summer 2023.